© Copyright 2023 - All rights reserved.

The contents of this book may not be reproduced, duplicated, or transmitted without direct written permission from the author. Under no circumstances will any legal responsibility or blame be held against the publisher for any reparation, damages, or monetary loss due to the information herein, either directly or indirectly.

This book is a work of fiction. Names, characters, and incidents are either the product of the author's imagination or are used fictitiously. Any resemblance to actual persons living or dead, business establishments, events, or locales is entirely coincidental.

Legal Notice: This book is Copyright protected. This is only for personal use. You cannot amend, distribute, sell, use, quote, or paraphrase any part of this book's content without the author's consent.

Disclaimer Notice: Please note the information contained within this document is for educational and entertainment purposes only. Every attempt has been made to provide accurate, up-to-date, reliable, and complete information. No warranties of any kind are expressed or implied. Readers acknowledge that the author is not rendering legal, financial, medical, or professional advice. The content of this book has been derived from various sources. Please consult a licensed professional before attempting any techniques outlined in this book.

By reading this document, the reader agrees that under no circumstances is the author responsible for any losses, direct or indirect, which are incurred as a result of the use of the information contained within this document, including, but not limited to, —errors, omissions, or inaccuracies. For information regarding permission, email the author at kisaboyun@gmail.com.

DEDICATION

A life lesson rolled into a fun story dedicated to her grandchildren and all the grandparents and grandchildren who have tried and failed to pull one over them.

Let her know what you think about this book by emailing kisaboyun@gmail.com. She promises never to spam your inbox.

DETECTIVE GRANDMA

THE BUSTED BROCCOLI PLOT

A.S.K. AYNUR

It was a big weekend for Lana the Llama and Shaggy the Sheep. Why?
Because they were going to stay with Grandma the Goat.

They loved staying with Grandma the Goat, not just because she was fun and let them do things, they weren't allowed to do at home... like put their hooves up on the coffee table!

They also loved staying with her because it meant they would be having a taste of their favorite meal in the world...
Grandma Goat's famous sausage roast.

Sausages.
Mashed potatoes.
Onion stuffing.
Thick, steaming gravy.
It was all delicious

'Well... almost all of it is delicious,' said Lana on the way to Grandma's house.

'What do you mean 'almost'?' asked Shaggy.

'The broccoli. I hate broccoli!' Lana said.

'Oh well. You can just hide it or something. I'm sure Grandma won't notice,' said Shaggy.

'Good idea,' said Lana. 'It's not like she's a detective or something, is it?'

Lana and Shaggy squealed with excitement.

Grandma had just placed a hot pile of food in front of each of them.

There it all was...

The sausages.

The mashed potatoes.

The onion stuffing.

The thick steaming gravy.

... and the broccoli.

'Gross,' whispered Lana.

'Now, you two,' said Grandma. 'I don't want to see any waste. Clean plates, please.'

'Yes, Grandma,' said Lana and Shaggy.

Shaggy ate everything very happily.
MUNCH, CRUNCH, CHOMP.

Lana, on the other hand, really didn't want to eat her broccoli. She tried hiding it under her stuffing... but her stuffing wasn't big enough to hide it.

She tried to hide it under her mashed potatoes... but then she started eating her mash and realized the hiding place was disappearing... into her mouth!

Through all this, Lana was sure Grandma hadn't noticed what she was trying to do.
But she had.

'Children, please excuse me for a moment,' said Grandma as she stood up from her chair and left the room, Lana took her chance.

She turned around and scraped the broccoli into the plant pot behind her.

Both Lana and Shaggy's plates were now empty.

'FINISHED!' they called.

'Are you indeed?' said Grandma.

She appeared from the kitchen holding a magnifying glass.

'Now... we're going to play a little game called Detective Grandma,' said Grandma.

'I thought you said she wasn't a detective,' whispered Shaggy.

'Looks like I was wrong,' replied Lana, panicking.

'I'm going to look around with my magnifying glass,' said Grandma. 'Whoever has eaten every last bit of their dinner will be allowed to play with my magnifying glass as a prize... anybody who hasn't...

WON'T!'

'Uh oh,' thought Lana.

First, Grandma spied over their empty plates.

Shaggy was first.

'Hmmm,' she said. 'A few crumbs of stuffing, but I shall allow that.'

'Phew,' said Shaggy.

Lana was next.

'Interesting,' said Grandma. 'A spotless plate. How suspicious.'

Lana gulped

Next, Grandma searched under the table.
"Nothing here. So far, so good," she said

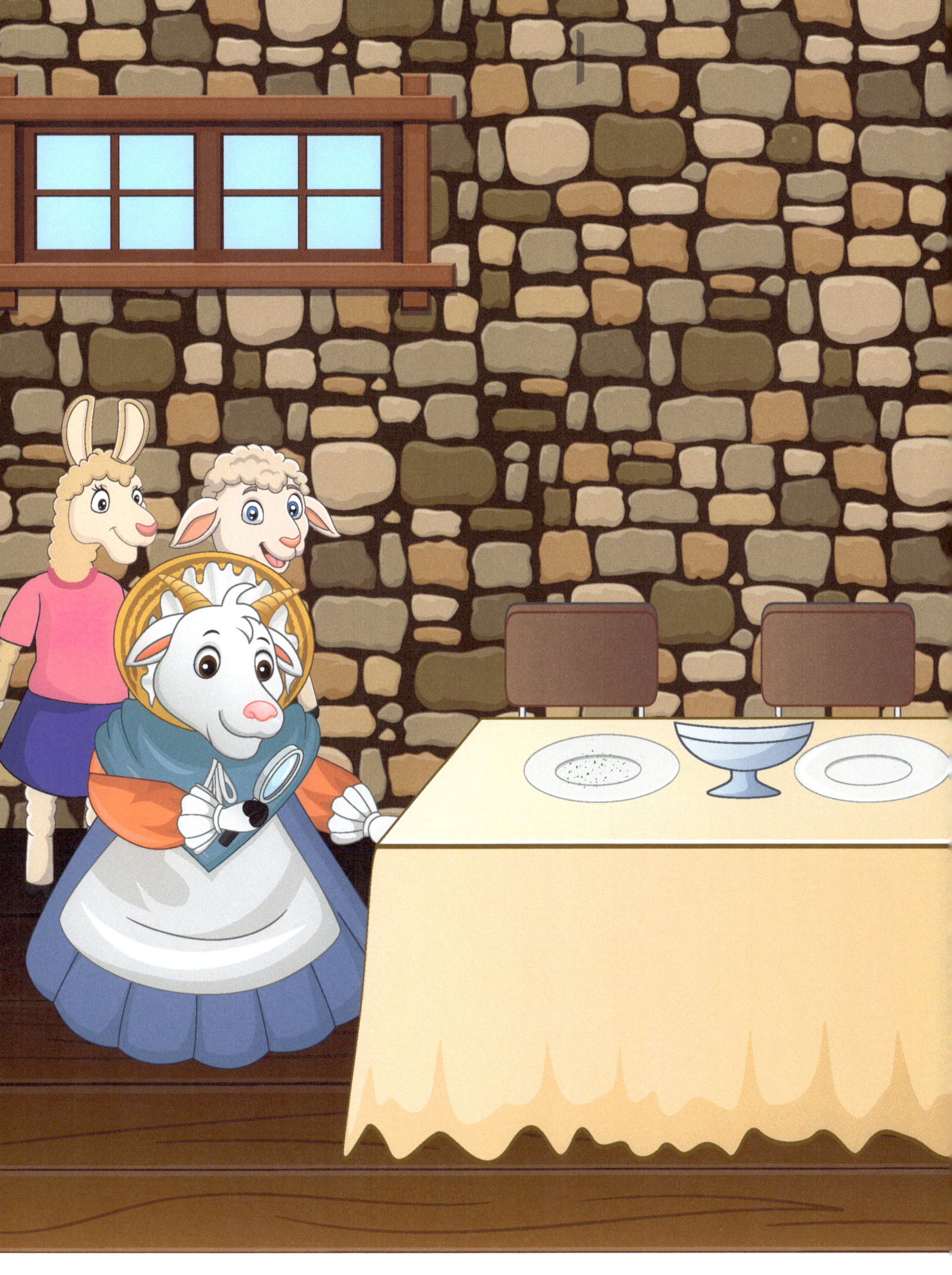

Then she searched inside the grandfather clock.
'Not a whiff of uneaten food here,' said Grandma.

And then... she saw the plant pot.

She crept up to it.

She got closer...

and CLOSER...

and CLOSER, until...

'OK, STOP!' yelled Lana.

'Something to confess, my dear?' asked Grandma.

'I'm sorry,' Lana said, pulling the broccoli from the plant pot.

'I didn't eat my broccoli. I'm sorry,

OK!'

Grandma was surprisingly calm.

'It's OK, dear,' said Grandma. 'I know you don't like broccoli. But instead of telling me and being honest... you lied.

You should never lie.

Do you know why?'

'Because it's wrong?' said Lana.

'Indeed, it is,' said Grandma. 'But also, when you lie... you always get found out eventually. And that is always much worse than if you had told the truth to begin with. It didn't feel nice to be found out, did it?'

'No,' said Lana.

'Promise never to lie to me again?' asked Grandma.

'I promise,' said Lana.

And I'm pleased to say it was a promise that Lana kept.

About the Author

Accidental author A.S.K. Aynur holds a Forensic Medicine Cert., Cert. in Early Childhood Education & Care Competency, and a Diploma in Counselling.

She is also a Paediatric Hypnosis Coach, Parents Coach, Kids Coach, ICF Accredited Life Coach, and Speaker. Despite her struggles to read and not having the ambition to write as a child, she became a best-selling author in 2020 with her first book.

That she has many strings to her bow is no surprise to anybody who knows her, as she is a serial entrepreneur. She describes her mind as very active and uses writing to get her ideas out and focus her thoughts. Her inspirations come from far and wide. She looks to world events, real-life stories, personal experiences, and the work of other writers.

Through her writing, she hopes to impress on her readers that, whatever life throws at you, there is always a funny side. She also aims to help parents teach their children good values through entertaining tales.

www.ingramcontent.com/pod-product-compliance
Lightning Source LLC
Chambersburg PA
CBHW042314280426
43661CB00101B/1254